Color Psych

CW00469874

Profit from The Psychology of Color:
Discover the Meaning and Effects of Color

Richard G. Lewis

Download a FREE infographic of Color Psychology here:

https://richardglewis.com/color-psychology-infographic

ISBN: 979-8-7305-7062-7

DEDICATION

To My Wonderful Wife, Son, and Family.

CONTENTS

INTRODUCTION

The study of the psychological effect of color on the human mind is a fascinating subject[1]. It is amazing how differently we react when exposed to different colors[2].

Color consultants believe that the colors used in the design of any object or environment (e.g., a website) can have a significant impact on the emotions and performance of people within that environment[3]. People respond, even at a psychological level, to colors[4].

Based upon fundamentals in color psychology, with years of research by color psychologists, the characteristics of certain colors have been identified to cause an emotional response in people[4]. This was done by studying the response from hundreds of thousands of test subjects around the world in order to isolate how certain colors make us feel.

The effect that color has on human emotions can be profound. Researchers have studied the biological perception of color, the relationships between color and emotion, and how different colors can be used to affect mood and behavior in predictable ways[5].

Many researchers believe that the perception of color is biologically based. However, the perceptions of these colors may affect our emotions and reactions based on cultural, psychological, and age-related influences[1].

Color sensitivity has been established to occur differently in different species. It is dependent on four properties fundamental to the discrimination of color: (i) wavelength discrimination, (ii) metamerism in color mixture, (iii) sensitivity to color and contrast, and (iv) a response consistency between the recognition of colors[6].

The sensitivity to color is defined by a species' "color space"; which for humans is based on three dimensions and is, therefore, "trichromatic"[7]. Humans are highly influenced by the environment into which any color has been presented[3].

Throughout history, color has always been associated with the emotions found in humans; we can be described as "green with envy" or "feeling blue". While some people are described as viewing the world "through rose-colored spectacles", others can be seen as "purple with fury"[8].

Researchers also believe that color is perceived not only biologically but emotionally and can instigate actual physiological reaction patterns within us[3, 4].

These connections are based on cultural differences, as well. While colors may have significance and representations in one culture, they may have little significance or completely different representations in another culture[9].

Researchers have tried to use the idea of *synesthesia* to explain the perception of some colors in humans. Synesthesia is an idea that the reaction to one stimulus somehow has a direct connection to the reaction of another stimulus[10].

As an example, they state that dark colors are often used to describe heaviness, while reds and oranges may be used to describe warmth. "Heavy" is then extrapolated to imply negative, and "warmth" would mean comfortable and positive[5]. With this connection, dark colors could imply negative thoughts, while red colors could imply positive[11].

Regardless of the origin of the sense or emotions which are related to color, it has been found that color is ordered on a preferential scale by humans[9]. An individual may prefer green over red, and in turn, red over blue, and blue over black, and so on[1].

Most humans can tell you their preferential order for colors. Humans can usually also relate their preferential order of objects as well[12].

Overall, adults preferred the color blue, followed by red, green, brown, yellow, and black. Children, on the other hand, prefer the colors red and yellow while the preference for blue and green increases over time[12].

The "anti-colors", black and white, were ranked quite low in all the groups[9]. This is found to be consistent across most studies conducted in Western societies. Children and adults ranked their emotions differently, as well[2]. While both groups generally ranked happiness and surprise the highest, followed by the four negative emotions: anger, sadness, fear, and aversion[12].

Tests have found that humans can order preferential colors and can match these colors to emotions. The discovery of the correlation between colors and emotions and their effect on humans is not new[13].

Although color psychology is a relatively new area of scientific research, ancient civilizations believed in the influence of color on humans; the ancient Chinese, Egyptians, and Indians believed in *chromotherapy*[14].

In ancient Egypt, patients would be color-diagnosed and then sent to an appropriately colored room to heal[14]. Recently, restaurants are said to implement the use of yellows and reds to stimulate the appetite (e.g., McDonald's, Burger King, Pizza Hut, etc.)[9] while hospitals have green rooms to soothe patients during their recovery and 'health' products tend to use light greens, turquoise, or aquamarine (e.g., toothpastes, mouth washes, etc.)[15].

Red has been found to stimulate the nervous system and increase breathing rates and boost skin and blood cell regeneration[16]. Consequently, it is recommended to use red when an individual wants to increase energy.

Orange is said to boost appetite and stimulate communication [17]. Therefore, orange is recommended for use in social living spaces and dining rooms[9].

Studies using yellow concluded that it increased mental stimulation, and boosted alertness, and IQ levels[18]. It is recommended to use yellow in an environment in which creativity needs to be enhanced[9].

Green has been found to reduce stress[15] and to be the easiest color on the eyes as its wavelength is the only one that comes into focus when human eyes are at rest[19].

Blue has been used in studies to relax muscles, lower blood pressure, and to calm hyperactive children[20].

Purple comes from the blue part of the spectrum and is said to provide some relaxation for subjects[9]. In addition, purple is often associated with spirituality, and has a soothing effect[21]. Purple should be used when a subject wants to relax and perhaps sleep[22].

Pink also has a calming effect on subjects and is used in some state prisons to calm aggressive prisoners. However, prolonged exposure can have a progressively opposite effect[23].

Yellows and reds have been found to provide subjects with an increase in energy and creativity[24]. On the other hand, exposure to blues, pinks, and purples are good for calming people down[9, 20, 22].

While it has been found that adults tend to connect the feeling of happiness with the color of yellow, it still does not remain high on the preferential scale for adults[25].

Orange boosts appetite while encouraging communication[17]. Whereas it has been shown that yellows and oranges provide the most stimulating and creative environments, adults still rank these low in the preferential scale[4].

Blues and greens are still highly preferred by the adult population, possibly because it provides a calming influence[9]. Since green is the easiest color on the human eye, it may be beneficial to use greens. It will help you get your prospects to spend a long time reading all your sales copy or information[19].

Since greens and blues are also calming and easy on the eyes, these would most likely be the most positive colors to use in the adult work place as green is also found to stimulate growth and balance emotions and is found to be highly preferred by adults[9].

Hues in the red area of the color spectrum are typically viewed as "warm", active, and exciting. Hues in the blue and green range are typically viewed as "cool", soothing, and passive. Physiological tests have revealed similar responses. It is claimed that red hues increase bodily tension and stimulate the autonomic nervous system, while "cool" hues release tension[26].

An increasing number of studies link colors to specific responses. One study found that sporting performances improved in blue rooms[27, 28], while another study found that babies cry more frequently in yellow rooms[29]. Pink ("drunk tank pink") is used by many law enforcement agencies in their detention cells to calm prisoners[23].

Note: Color, as seen on screen, is not absolute, every monitor gives out a slightly different version of each color, and this is most visible on older computer monitors.

Overleaf are some common cultural connotations attached to colors in Western cultures, particularly in the United States of America:

BLACK

Black represents the absolute boundary beyond which life exists, and so expresses the idea of nothingness or extinction. Black is the 'No' to the 'Yes' of white. White and black are the two extremes; the Alpha and the Omega, the beginning and the end.

Image 1 Yin-yang symbol

With its strong associations of renunciation, surrender, and relinquishment, black is often seen as a negative color, but it can emphasize and enforce the characteristics of any color it surrounds. Consequently, black is an excellent color to give emphasis.

Pretty much anything goes with black; it sets specific contrast associations when paired with other colors.

Black can be an extremely influential color; along with grey, it is the top choice for business suits. It is the color of mystery, of things not yet revealed. It is a strong, unequivocal color. Black is a polarizing color that suggests an opposite: empty/full, dark/light, evil/good.

Image 2 8 Ball

Black also carries positive and negative connotations, and you should consider its use judiciously. On the one hand, black can be sophisticated, elegant, and representative of modernism - this is an association especially true for wealthy, achievement-orientated women.

Image 3 Limousine

On the other hand, it can symbolize corruption, emptiness, and depression. For many socio-economic groups and cultures, black is the color of mourning, grief, and death. Suggested uses: classic, expressive products (diamonds), jewelry, gadgets, fashion items, etc.

Image 4 Little Black Dress

Black has the following cultural associations: modernity, power, sophistication, formality, elegance, wealth, mystery, style, evil, death, fear, anonymity, anger, sadness, remorse, mourning, unhappiness, mystery. According to some researchers, people in many cultures have an automatic negative perception of the color black.

Image 5 Pentagram

BLUE

lue is the color of calmness, relaxation, and unity. Symbolically, blue is the color of the sky and ocean; that is why there is a basic human physiological need to see the color blue often. Looking at blues relaxes the central nervous system and blood pressure.

Image 6 Blue sea and sky

The psychological associations with blue are those of tranquility, contentment, gratification, and being at peace. Although men favor a darker shade of blue, for women, blue is the preferred color for evoking a soothing, calming, and tranquility.

Image 7 Bath salts

Blue is the best performing color for business websites, any content that explains complicated issues, banks (blue can evoke trustworthiness), spiritual and sporting products.

Image 8 Barclays Bank

Image 9 Ford Motor Company

It is no accident that so many corporate color schemes incorporate blue; it is the number one consumer favorite color. And, along with black and grey, blue is a favorite color for business suits as well as the most popular color for uniforms. Blue is also the color of your local policeman's uniform, which suggests power and authority but also inspires confidence, a sense of safety, and trustworthiness.

For some cultures, blue is the color that wards off evil spirits - the ultimate color metaphor for protection.

Image 10 Private security badge

Blue has the following cultural associations: seas, skies, peace, unity, harmony, tranquility, calmness, coolness, confidence, water, ice, loyalty, conservatism, dependability, cleanliness, technology, winter, depression, coldness, idealism, obscenity, ice, tackiness, winter, etc. Blue is universally the best color for business as it has the most positive and fewest negative cultural associations across various cultures.

Strange facts: Blue creates an optical impression that objects are farther away than they really are. In numerous tests, a blue-colored environment improved workplace productivity.

BROWN

Brown is symbolic of roots and family security. Brown is a darkened mixture of red and yellow, with reduced qualities of these colors. The impulses of brown are not as violent or volatile as red and not as restless as yellow. Yet, the color has subtle, warm, welcoming, and sensuous qualities.

Image 11 Chocolate cake

When Brown is favored, it suggests an increased need for physical ease and sensuous contentment or release from discomfort (e.g., products and services that require trustworthiness, such as couriers, pain-relief products, and mental health).

Image 12 UPS logo

Brown is the color of the Earth, roots, and the giving of life. It is also linked with wealth and a subtle but expensive taste (e.g., premium cigars, gourmet coffee, luxury chocolates, etc.).

Image 13 Cohiba cigars

It is a secure color, a home-grown color, a grounded color. However, brown is also associated with things that are dirty and unclean. The enormous appeal of chocolate, beer, and coffee has given brown a bit of a boost in popularity, evoking qualities of comfort, and a satisfying aroma.

Image 14 Gloria Jean's Coffee logo

Brown has the following cultural associations: calm, depth, natural organisms, nature, richness, rustic, stability, tradition, anachronism, boorishness, dirt, dullness, filth, heaviness, poverty, roughness, etc.

Image 15 Brown iron oxide

GRAY

G ray is the color of neutrality, free from stimulus, non-involvement, or concealment; uncommitted and uninvolved.

Image 16 Gray t-shirt

Good for backgrounds, or non-intrusive elements, gray is good as a canvas for emphasizing a key color or design element.

Image 17 Apple logo

Gray has the following cultural associations: elegance, humility, respect, reverence, stability, subtlety, timelessness, wisdom, anachronism, boredom, decay, decrepitude, dullness, dust, pollution, urban sprawl, etc.

Image 18 Gray Nike sneakers

GREEN

Green is the color often associated with a desire for improved conditions, the search for better health and social reform. It is a color that the person who possesses or wishes to possess high levels of self-esteem responds to strongly. It is the color of nature, a sign of growth, the harbinger of spring, and warmer weather. Green represents optimism, good luck, freshness, fertility, and suggests that things are getting better.

Image 19 Green party politics

As the color of money, it has strong associations with finance, business, economic stability, and entitlements. There is a hint of green (especially British racing green) rooted in traditional, classic, and affluent products, services, and past times.

Image 20 Jaguar logo

Green is the most restful color on the eye, and human eyes can discern more shades of green than any other color (a biological consequence of our outdoor living past)

.

Greens are used in the health and finance markets as we associate green with outdoor pursuits and healthy living. That is why we view shades of green as trustworthy and calming. Also, green is traditionally the color of money in most of the world's economies.

Image 21 A 100-dollar bill

Green has its downside. Green is linked with envy, sickness, slime, and decaying food. Yellow or green chartreuse is the second most hated color in North America. The best-favored shades of green across all consumer lines, including gender, are the blue-greens, such as aquamarine.

Image 22 Bulgari's Aqua Marine

One group of people that respond very well to green is the influencers (i.e., aficionados, devotees, and mavens). Those opinion-leaders to whom prospective customers go to for advice.

Green is good for high-ticket items, aspirational goods (e.g., Rolex, Jaguar, Harrods, etc.), and spiritual or natural products (e.g., The Body Shop).

Image 23 The Body Shop logo

Green has the following cultural associations: nature, spring, fertility, youth, the environment, wealth, money, good luck, vigor, generosity, go, grass, aggression, inexperience, envy, misfortune, jealousy, illness, greed, etc.

Image 24 Go sign

ORANGE

Orange may suggest fire, vitality, warmth, and energy, which are all good associations. However, it is the most detested color by Americans. It is more popular in Europe and has a particularly strong appeal in Latino and French cultures (e.g., Orange Telecom is a French company).

Image 25 Orange logo

The research suggests if you are going to use orange, it is best tolerated when you are evoking a natural association like sunshine, oranges, carrots, etc. That, or go for a deeper orange.

Image 26 Orange logo

One group of people that respond very well to orange devotees, enthusiasts, and mavens). Use orange for mavens and influencers if you need to get a message across. Harley Davidson is an excellent example of brand devotees spreading the word of the brand.

Image 27 Harley-Davidson logo

Because orange is found in the wavelength between red (the color of blood, the most emotive of colors), and yellow (the most stimulating of colors), orange is the ultimate "action" color; established as a motivating color for sports teams, etc.

Image 28 Orioles logo

This has been proven to be the best color to use if you want to get people to take action.

Image 29 'Add To Cart' button

Orange has the following cultural associations: Buddhism, energy, balance, heat, fire, enthusiasm, flamboyance, playfulness, aggression, arrogance, flamboyance, gaudiness, over-emotion, warning, danger, fire, etc.

PINK

Pink makes most people think of baby girls.

Image 30 Baby girl

Along with yellow, pinks are considered the warmest and most cheerful of colors; pink is the more popular of the two.

Image 31 Love Pink

Soft pink generates simple, uncomplicated emotions. In fact, soft pink is so successful at eliciting gentler reactions that it is the color of the walls in some prison cells.

Image 32 Drunk Tank pink

Hot pink, just like most fluorescent colors, is low in popular appeal.

Image 33 Hot pink fluorescent lighting

Suggested uses would include girls' clothes and toys, comedy items and themes, gay products, and services.

Note: Pink has few cultural associations but is associated with gay culture in the West.

Image 34 Gay t-shirt

PURPLE

Purple is a complex color, not just in terms of its associations but also in terms of the reactions different people have to it.

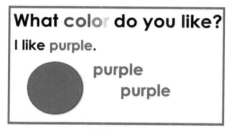

Image 35 I like purple

Interestingly, it is also the hardest color for the human eye to discriminate.

Image 36 Gradient between red and blue

It can be intense and ephemeral like the final glow of the sunset, or brave like a purple heart.

Image 37 Purple Heart

It is often associated with magic, royalty, palm reading, clairvoyance, the occult, and horoscopes.

Image 38 Horoscope.com

It can be cool and full of authority and rich. Purple suggests intelligence and creativity, but it also suggests cruelty. In some cultures, purple is the color of mourning.

If the purple is on the blue side of the color spectrum, people tend to associate it with mystical qualities; if it is on the red side, the associations are more sensual.

Image 39 Curves Fitness Company

Red purples grab people's attention more effectively than blue purples. Those between the ages of 18 to 29 are especially partial to this color.

Purples are used by online dating agencies because they tend to put us in a warm, receptive mood.

Image 40 Cupid PLC

Perhaps most interesting of all is the fact that psychologists have recently proven that light purple is the color most conducive to making customers feel least resistant to spending money. Therefore, it can be recommended that you at least use this color on the pre-pay or payment page of your web site.

Image 41 Yahoo!

Purple has the following cultural associations: sensuality, spirituality, creativity, wealth, royalty, nobility, ceremony, mystery, wisdom, enlightenment, arrogance, flamboyance, gaudiness, mourning, profanity, exaggeration, confusion, etc.

RED

R ed means "stop". The 'Don't press the red button!' sign, strongly suggests that you should avoid using red call-to-action buttons. Studies suggest that users hesitate for longer before pressing a red button or even avoid it altogether.

Image 42 Red 'Buy Now' button

Red promotes images emotions of excitement, drama, urgent passion, strengths, assertiveness, and an appetite stimulant (used by McDonald's, Coca Cola, Pizza Hut, and Burger King).

Image 43 McDonald's logo

It is the color of Valentine's Day heart, love, the red apple, and fire trucks. It promises excitement and good times.

Image 44 Red Heart

Red is also the color of the devil. Lots of casinos use red signs (often with yellow) and red lighting because people are happier to risk their money under red light.

Image 45 Casino sign

In most commercial applications, it seems people respond best to red when it is used as an accent or highlight. Strong preferences for reds are linked demographically to those who feel most secure - both economically and personally. Men favor yellow reds; women prefer real reds.

Image 46 Pinterest logo

Physiologically, red makes blood pressure, pulse, and respiratory system rates go up; it is an energy expanding color. Reds are used extensively in the pornography industry because they tend to put us in an excitable mood (but only for a short period of time before it becomes irritating).

Red's associations are with vitality, activity, desire, appetite, and craving. Symbolically, red is blood, conquest, masculinity, the flame of the human spirit.

Image 47 Winning rugby team

Red creates the impulse towards active doing; towards sport, struggle, competition, eroticism, enterprising productivity, the intensity of experience and forms of living; sex, sport, fast cars (e.g., Ferrari red), etc.

Image 48 Red sports car

Red has the following cultural associations: passion, strength, energy, fire, love, sex, excitement, speed, heat, leadership, masculinity, power, danger, fire, gaudiness, blood, war, anger, revolution, radicalism, aggression, stop, etc.

VIOLET

Violet, being a combination of red and blue, unifies the heat of red and the gentler tone of blue.

Image 49 Violet flower

Light purples are mystical, suggesting sensitive intimacy, union, enchantment, desire, and reality. Violet represents a longing for the wishes to be fulfilled and a desire to charm others.

Image 50 'MYSTIC'

Violet can be identified as an intimate, erotic blending, or it can lead to an intuitive and sensitive understanding.

Image 51 Parma Violet Candle Jar

Because it is so strongly associated with the idea of the world as a magical place, and the need for wish fulfillment, a preference for violet can communicate some degree of vulnerability or insecurity, perhaps a need for approval.

Image 52 Floralia

Suggested uses: dating websites, or comforting products, such as chocolate or bath products.

WHITE

White is the color of the dove of peace, crispness, tidiness, innocence, moral purity, and cleanliness.

Image 53 Wedding dress

It can also suggest sterility and blandness.

Image 54 White doctor's coat

Although it is a neutral color, pure white is considered a brilliant color capable of producing optical fatigue due to it being highly visible to the human eye.

Image 55 Apple iPhone

White has the following cultural associations: reverence, purity, snow, peace, innocence, cleanliness, simplicity, security, humility, marriage, sterility, winter, coldness, clinical, surrender, cowardice, fearfulness, unimaginative, etc.

YELLOW

Yellow is primarily the color of happiness, cheerful mood, expansiveness, lack of inhibition. It is the welcome warmth of the sun and the glow of a spiritual halo.

Image 56 Sunshine symbol

While calming and relaxing, the color dares suggest a desire for change; that things are never quite at rest. People who favor yellow may be very productive, but that productivity often occurs in fits and starts.

Image 57 Tour de France's Yellow Jersey

When yellow is used with black, it suggests warning - think stinging insects, traffic caution signs, and labels for hazardous materials.

Image 58 Biohazard sign

Due to its wavelength, yellow is the first color the eye processes. It is bright, sunny, powerful, welcoming, cheerful, and the color most visible to the human eye.

Image 59 Sunflower

Lots of its associations are positive, such as deities with glowing halos and golden hair, enlightenment, and precious metals. It evokes a few negative responses as well, in associations with dishonesty, cowardice, legalism, betrayal, and caution.

Image 60 Lifejacket

Yellow has the following cultural associations: sunlight, joy, happiness, optimism, idealism, wealth (gold), summer, hope, cowardice, illness (quarantine), hazards, dishonesty, avarice, weakness, etc.

Image 61 Ferrari logo

Suggested uses: Children's products, holiday, tourism, etc.

CULTURAL DIFFERENCES

Various cultures see color differently. In India, blue is associated with Krishna (a positive association), green with Islam, red with purity (used as a wedding color), and brown with mourning.

Image 62 Pakistan flag

In most Asian cultures, yellow is the imperial color with many of the same cultural associations as purple in the West.

Image 63 Chinese Imperial Dress

In China, red is symbolic of celebration, good luck, and prosperity, white is symbolic of mourning and death, while wearing a green hat means a man's wife is cheating on him!

Image 64 Chinese lanterns

In Europe, colors are more strongly associated with political parties than they are in North America.

Image 65 USA Political Parties

Red, white, and blue, together are still the biggest, best-selling combo for packaging in the US.

Image 66 Red, white & blue packaging

In many countries, black is synonymous with conservatism (even fascism), red with socialism (and communism), and green is immediately associated with ecology and environmental issues.

Image 67 The Green Party

THE MAGIC COLORS

The favorite color combination on the internet is blue and yellow. 'Blue for Business' is a rule followed by many companies that want to give a serious, trustworthy, corporate image.

Image 68 Skype for Business

This is because everybody reacts well to blue; being the color of the sky and the sea, it evokes a feeling of well-being. It can also promote a pensive, thoughtful state of mind; the mood you want a potential customer to be in (a decision-making state of mind) such as when you are considering buying something.

Image 69 Chase Business Credit Card

On the other hand, yellow, due to its wavelength, is the color that our eyes find hardest to cope with. Yellow is the color that attracts out attention the most – that is why nature makes dangerous animals (snakes), and insects (bees and wasps) yellow on black. And also, motorway signs are often black on yellow to capture our maximum attention.

Therefore, yellow should be used sparingly and for emphasis only.

For one-off sales and impulse buying the magic colors, when used judiciously, are aquamarine and orange.

Image 70 Aquamarine & Orange color combination

Aquamarine is the color of the sea (an element that most people are comfortable and positive about). It is a color that promotes decision-making and considered (along with the color of the earth; brown) as the most 'trustworthy' of all colors. Trustworthiness and credibility are two of the most important attributes potential customers look for in a vendor.

Image 71 Amazon 'Buy Now' button

Orange gives the user a sense of independence and is the color that promotes decisive action. This is the exact mood you want a potential customer to be in when it comes to the crucial 'call-to-action' buying decision.

CHOOSE YOUR MOOD

Color speaks to the subconscious, evokes meanings and feelings and moods, and has an incredible ability to influence buying behavior.

Depending on the mood you want to convey and the target market you want to attract, you can choose a color palette that will help achieve the optimum online environment.

Use two or three colors (no more than three colors). Fewer colors make for a stronger statement and tend not to over-stimulate or tax your prospects. Using three shades of the same color is often more effective than using three different colors. In e-commerce, color is a clear case where less is often more.

- **Traditional**: burgundy, teal, navy, dark green, gold, plum, slate blue, vanilla.
- **Nurturing**: peach, honey yellows, warm rose, cream, lilac, baby blue, soft green.
- **Romantic**: pink, rose, sage green, lilac, antique white, cameo blue.
- **Tranquil**: blue, blue-green, lavender, aquamarine, mauve, light grey.
- **Contemplative**: neutral grey, beige, taupe, off-white with colored accents.
- Whimsical: red, bright blue, mid yellow, green, orange, periwinkle, vibrant pink.
- **Sensuous**: warm red, mango, plum purple, hot pink, gold, deep blue, chocolate.

CONCLUSION

I wrote this book as a guide to all Internet Marketers because I think it is essential that we in the industry understand the underused psychological influence of color.

Changing the colors on your sales page or website won't suddenly bring in millions of dollars but there is no doubt that a change of color may well result in a change of mood in the viewer; it's how you use that power that can determine your profitability.

The challenge for you as an Internet Marketers is to understand the theories of color and to use them in a profitable but professional and ethical way.

Well, those are the theories, now go turn them into cash ☺

Profit from Persuasion,

Richard G Lewis

Richard G. Lewis
https://richardglewis.com

If you enjoyed this book you might like to download a handy infographic on the same subject here: https://richardglewis.com/color-psychology-infographic

ABOUT THE AUTHOR

Richard G. Lewis is a research psychologist, business consultant and author. Richard helps other business owners, internet marketers and copywriters to understand the power of psychology and persuasion, so they can change their lives for the better and start making a living online.

Richard G. Lewis

Since 1998 he has helped develop over 70 e-commerce projects, designing the web architecture, writing the sales copy and marketing plans for all those brands.

Richard has also written numerous research papers, e-books and books, including: "Pre Cursor" (2010), "Fortune Cookie" (2009) and the bestseller, "The Small Business Guide to the Internet" (1998).

He has degrees in both Business and Computing. He is also a Fellow of the Chartered Institute of Marketing as well as an expert in e-commerce as recognized by the UK Expert Witness Directory.

Note: Richard is available for consultancy at consultancy@richardglewis.com

REFERENCES

[1] Kurt, S. and Osueke, K.K. (2014) "The Effects of Color on the Moods of College Students". *SAGE Open* 4, 2158244014525423

[2] Abegaz, T., Dillon, E., and Gilbert, J.E. (2015) "Exploring affective reaction during user interaction with colors and shapes". *Procedia Manufacturing* 3, 5253-5260

[3] Jalil, N.A., Yunus, R.M., and Said, N.S. (2012) "Environmental Colour Impact upon Human Behaviour: A Review". *Procedia - Social and Behavioral Sciences* 35, 54-62

[4] Jain, A. (2017) "Psychology of Colours in Building Design". *International Journal of Engineering Science and Computing* 7, 10394-10396

[5] Wise, B.K. and Wise, J.A. (1988) "The human factors of color in environmental design: A critical review".

[6] Saunders, B. (1998) "What is colour?". *British Journal of Psychology* 89, 697-704

[7] Jameson, K.A. (2009) "Human Potential for Tetrachromacy". *Glimpse: The Art+ Science of Seeing* 2, 82-91

[8] Jonauskaite, D., Parraga, C.A., Quiblier, M., and Mohr, C. (2020) "Feeling Blue or Seeing Red? Similar Patterns of Emotion Associations With Colour Patches and Colour Terms". *Iperception* 11, 2041669520902484-2041669520902484

[9] Church, T. (2010) The psychology of color and its effects on home and work environments.

[10] Safran, A.B. and Sanda, N. (2015) "Color synesthesia. Insight into perception, emotion, and consciousness". *Curr Opin Neurol* 28, 36-44

[11] Meyers-Levy, J. and Peracchio, L.A. (1995) "Understanding the effects of color: How the correspondence between available and required resources affects attitudes". *Journal of consumer research* 22, 121-138

12   Jonauskaite, D., Mohr, C., Antonietti, J.-P., Spiers, P.M., Althaus, B., Anil, S., and Dael, N. (2016) "Most and least preferred colours differ according to object context: new insights from an unrestricted colour range". *PLoS One* 11, e0152194

13   Ou, L.-C., Luo, M.R., Woodcock, A., and Wright, A. (2004) "A study of colour emotion and colour preference. Part I: Colour emotions for single colours". *Color Research & Application* 29, 232-240

14   Azeemi, S.T.Y. and Raza, S.M. (2005) "A critical analysis of chromotherapy and its scientific evolution". *Evid Based Complement Alternat Med* 2, 481-488

15   van den Bosch, M. and Ode Sang, Å. (2017) "Urban natural environments as nature-based solutions for improved public health - A systematic review of reviews". *Environmental research* 158, 373-384

16   Gilston, A. and Privitera, G.J. (2015) "A "Healthy" Color: Information About Healthy Eating Attenuates the "Red Effect"". *Glob J Health Sci* 8, 56-61

17   Spence, C. (2015) "On the psychological impact of food colour". *Flavour* 4, 21

18   Tao, B., Xu, S., Pan, X., Gao, Q., and Wang, W. (2015) "Personality trait correlates of color preference in schizophrenia". *Transl Neurosci* 6, 174-178

19   Thorpert, P. (2019) Green is not just green.

20   Minguillon, J., Lopez-Gordo, M.A., Renedo-Criado, D.A., Sanchez-Carrion, M.J., and Pelayo, F. (2017) "Blue lighting accelerates post-stress relaxation: Results of a preliminary study". *PLoS One* 12, e0186399-e0186399

21   Harmony, F. (2020) The meaning of purple. Violet color: symbolism and impact on humans. I'm all violet. https://mgmshop.ru/en/the-value-of-a-purple-color-purple-color-symbolism-and-influence-on-the-person/

22   Night, C. and Bates, W. (2011) *Do It Yourself - Natural Eyesight Improvement - Original and Modern Bates Method: with Better*

Eyesight Magazine by Ophthalmologist William H. Bates. CreateSpace Independent Publishing Platform

23   Genschow, O., Noll, T., Wänke, M., and Gersbach, R. (2015) "Does Baker-Miller pink reduce aggression in prison detention cells? A critical empirical examination". *Psychology, Crime & Law* 21, 482-489

24   Chapman, C. (2010) "Color theory for designers, part 1: The meaning of color". *Smashing magazine* 28, 2010

25   Fugate, J.M.B. and Franco, C.L. (2019) "What Color Is Your Anger? Assessing Color-Emotion Pairings in English Speakers". *Frontiers in psychology* 10, 206-206

26   Reetesh, V.S.A. (2017) *Word Power Made Handy, 2nd Edition*. S. Chand Publishing

27   Iwase, M. (2002) Sports and colors: the color effect of team shirts on basketball games. In *9th Congress of the International Colour Association*, pp. 413-417, International Society for Optics and Photonics

28   Xia, T., Song, L., Wang, T.T., Tan, L., and Mo, L. (2016) "Exploring the Effect of Red and Blue on Cognitive Task Performances". *Frontiers in Psychology* 7

29   O'connor, Z. (2011) "Colour psychology and colour therapy: Caveat emptor". *Color Research & Application* 36, 229-234

Printed in Great Britain
by Amazon

23561503R00039